Primers
Volume Seven

Primers
Volume Seven

Jade Cuttle
Antonia Taylor
Laura Varnam

Selected by Katie Hale

Nine
Arches
Press

Primers: Volume Seven
Jade Cuttle, Antonia Taylor, and Laura Varnam
Selected by Katie Hale

ISBN: 978-1-913437-98-5
eISBN: 978-1-913437-99-2

Cover design by Jane Commane.

First published August 2024 by:

Nine Arches Press
Unit 14, Sir Frank Whittle Business Centre,
Great Central Way, Rugby.
CV21 3XH
United Kingdom

www.ninearchespress.com

Printed on recycled paper in the United Kingdom
by Imprint Digital.

Nine Arches Press is supported using public funding
by Arts Council England.

Supported using public funding by
**ARTS COUNCIL
ENGLAND**

About the Editor:

Katie Hale is a novelist and poet, based in Cumbria. She won a Northern Debut Award for her poetry collection, *White Ghosts*, and is the author of two novels: *The Edge of Solitude* and *My Name is Monster*. She is a former MacDowell Fellow, and winner of the Palette Poetry Prize, Munster Chapbook Prize, and *Aesthetica* Creative Writing Prize. Her short fiction has been longlisted for the BBC National Short Story Award, and she has held Writer in Residence positions in numerous countries, including Australia, the US and Svalbard. Katie also mentors young writers through Writing Squad.

Contents

Laura Varnam

Foreword

The Primers poetry mentoring scheme began in 2015 with the objective of highlighting innovative debut poets who are yet to have had a full collection published. Primers runs biannually and has now published twenty-two new poets, with three finalists each time selected by a guest judge and receiving one-to-one mentoring and editing advice, all designed to take their poetry into print and out into the world.

The seventh call for submissions in 2023 introduced us to many new, talented poets. We were struck by the consistent quality and distinctiveness of voice in the poems and were intrigued to see how the submissions we had shortlisted might open up into a wider selection of poems.

The ten shortlisted poets didn't disappoint – and delivered a variety of themes, approaches and poetic forms. Often, these demonstrated their ability to craft poems which were in imaginative conversation with each other, whether formally or informally. With such rich, vital new poetry to choose from, there was much careful reading; selecting our three finalists for Primers was a challenging but thoroughly enjoyable process, and we're delighted to present here in this collection, the work of Jade Cuttle, Antonia Taylor, and Laura Varnam.

Jade Cuttle's poems of earth and Brownness are abundant in mud and loam and soil. From the start, we were struck by their grounding in the literal ground – how they use the physicality of the earth (what's buried in and what rises from it) to explore a Brown identity. We were also struck by how playful they are in their use of form. From lists to playscript, to scientific hypothesis and diagram, these are poems that are unafraid to metamorphose. Each poem is tightly crafted, but they give the appearance of growing organically from the page. Like a rich compost, they sprout fresh language, and embrace us with their burgeoning lexicon.

The musicality of Antonia Taylor's poems lets them slip lullingly into the ear – but within their flowing melody lie images at once beautiful and gut-punching. In *Making a Big Deal of Stuffed Vine Leaves*, Antonia Taylor explores her Cypriot heritage in ways that feel sometimes tenderly confessional, sometimes achingly political, often both. These are poems that don't give everything up on first reading. They open a door, show us some of the human joy and ache that lies inside. Read them again and again; each read is a hand offered for us to hold, to guide us further and further in.

In her poem sequence, *Grendel's Mother Bites Back*, Laura Varnam writes 'with' or 'towards' or 'in answer to' or perhaps 'opposite to' *Beowulf*. The poems incorporate Old English (with footnotes) to grapple with issues of translation, with explorations of who gets to be written about, by whom and in what way. Grendel's Mother herself is a force and a delight. There is a wry smile even in her very first word – but she is also both angry and impassioned, and full of regret as she takes the stage and refuses to relinquish the mic. She's a character and voice that stay with you, singing out into the dark long after you have stopped reading.

All three poets also impressed us with the ways in which they have embraced the process of mentoring and editing, and we are so pleased to have been part of their journey towards publication. Our thanks and admiration also to the seven other shortlisted poets Rebecca Ferrier, Bethany Handley, Erica Hesketh, Nashwa Nasreldin, Ilisha Thiru Purcell, Henry St Leger, and Caroline Stancer, whose engaging and innovative poems we admired. We also extend our thanks to those longlisted, whose new writing also caught our attention.

In this new volume, each poet in their own way unearths and peels back the layers of narrative, as only the best poems can. We are delighted to bring these three wonderful poets and their adventurous and distinctive new work to you.

Katie Hale and Jane Commane,
July 2024.

Jade Cuttle

Jade Cuttle is a BBC New Generation Thinker and former Arts Commissioning Editor at *The Times*, completing AHRC-funded research into British Nature Poets of Colour at Cambridge. Since her Masters in Poetry at UEA she has won a Northern Writers' Award, Arts Council and PRS Foundation grants, first place in BBC Proms Poetry Competition, National Poetry Competition longlisting and selection for Faber's Writing Chance. She's a Ledbury Critic and Poetry School tutor, anthologised by Carcanet and broadcast across the BBC. Her albums of poem-songs include *Algal Bloom* and *Orchid Duets*.

www.jadecuttle.co.uk @JadeCuttle

These poems explore my 'baptism into Brownness': a deeper shade to the skin I have always known. They are born from a solidarity I discover between soil and self: aesthetically in colour, historically in hierarchy, and ideologically in the history we both hold. Sometimes, this solidarity arises while mudlarking, searching between sewage for the forgotten shards of history, or rumbling soil of its rusty secrets while metal detecting. Other times, it surfaces while fighting sword and shield on the battlefield as a medieval re-enactor, sinking into mud and murky depths of time itself. Elsewhere, it is through nourishing the seeds of silted kinship that sprout while sleeping in my garden shed. While Georges Perec guided readers to 'see more flatly', and Robert Macfarlane encouraged readers to 'see more deeply', these poems offer an invitation to instead 'see more brownly'. They are also driven by a curiosity for linguistic invention that culminates in the creation of a *mossary*: a subversive glossary of eco-coinings. This *mossary* becomes a manifesto for rewilding language and thought, a fertilisation rather than flattening of biodiverse thought-paths. The *mossary* is interested in the coin aspect of coinage; in self-generating a poetic currency that carries the potential to counter colonial legacies (a *scriptocurrency*) and gain purchase in a historically exclusive genre.

Jade Cuttle

Mudlark

noun: /'mʌd.laːk/: a person who scavenges the mud
of a river for items of historical value; once a 19th-century
profession for destitute townsfolk; a *slob-dweller, skin-flint,*
or *snecklifter* of lumped coal, copper or bone; often children,
a *rust-urchin* or *gutter-snipe*; or women, a *dock-fairy, slag-
tenant* or *water-flirt*; now white middle-class sport; poaching
hair pin and pipe from the water's fist — knuckled and boned
by dock-bollards — the trophies of tidal uprising; a *pier-coloniser,
silt-flayer* or *land-stripper*; history's pickpocket or proofreader;
a journalist of junk; occasionally, a brown person who prowls
the shore in search of oneself; a *silt-grubbling* or *mud-goblin*;
a human-splinter at home with the shit and shards; a surgeon
of skeletal wasteland whose muscle slackens but never scars;
a coroner of stubbed-out dreams, guided by the ferrous gristle
of the foreshore: *river-slave* or *sludge-master,* we are all pilgrims
to the brown and broken; land-healers in training. So let us kneel
at this altar of silt and silence; moor our hearts between its shifting
plastic shores

sewage pin 1p mud siltspawn dead mouse 2p thimble comb Heinz can pipe wig curler 1p vape pen dice pin trolley ID plastic bag 青花 salthood cable syringe bottle cap 20p Lucozade fossilised tooth shoe sole pin rosary bead Walkers crisps keyboard ring bonehood 1p glass bottle sword pen cling film football 2p cigarette polystyrene dead fish 1p pin straw plate screw marble screw human-splinter tampon bolt kiln 1p Oyster card £1 pin nappy 5p cheesy puff E coli pipe bowl foil knife 2p spoon 回回青 chips earring dead eel banana iPhone pipe soilache pebble plastic stirrer Tesco bag foam rust buoy rope Bartmann jug pin 17th-century clay pipe Rolex doll sewage post-it note bolt 1p scissors clamp 5p bollard mouse pad 2p S aureus stapler teabag condom satchel £2 Asda bag pin copper debit card pipe Marlboro box waste brooch zombie river dinar sludgehood coal pot safety pin battery Sprite clamp 10p calculator biro Tetanus 1p oil plastic sores

Shore as stage: a one-act poem

After Samuel Beckett

ACT I

Scene I

Millennium Bridge, by Shakespeare's Globe Theatre, present day. **BROWN MUDLARK** *stoops over the silt. They use a scraper to work the shore, excavating bolts and other non-treasures with their hands. Enter* **WHITE MUDLARK** *with sanitiser, rubber gloves and knee pads.*

WHITE MUDLARK: What did you find?

BROWN MUDLARK *empties left pocket of seaweed-embroidered handcuffs, broken skulls of medieval bowls and a grave-shard of clay smoking pipes, snuffed into silence by the grout of a grubby tide.*

WHITE MUDLARK: Did you find anything else?

BROWN MUDLARK *empties right pocket of moss-lined fetters, rust-clasped fists of ferrous chunks, coins lodged in the faulty slot machine of mud, half-digested by the slow guts of ground.*

WHITE MUDLARK: What did you find, anything else?

BROWN MUDLARK *gestures beyond the dripping green horde to skeletons in mud and slavery of mind; footsteps of the forgotten, looping the edgelands of memory in an endless ghost-ramble.*

WHITE MUDLARK: Anything else did you find?

*Exit **BROWN MUDLARK** with a welly squelch of mud and muted revolt, brandishing a pilgrim badge sculpted not in silver but in silt.*

Why are you visiting this river?

There is no free movement
    except for clean white water:
anything else
    will snag at the first log:
detained underwater
    until skin turns soft
and kindly falls

        away.

Mossary - I

bonehood: skeletal truth uniting humans beneath and beyond the transitory shawl of skin

human-splinter: splintered version of humanhood, inherited through heritage, or acquired through grief or trauma

rust-urchin: person who scavenges the rust of a river for items of value

salthood: substance of selfhood that remains like salt in a glass when sludgehood (see below) is separated from the white residue of pretence

siltspawn: debris carried by a river, or offspring of a black person (derogatory)

sludgehood: undesirable residue or viscous waste-product of colonialism; stains perceptions of self or converts to poetic fuel

soilache: longing to relearn the touch of soil; to soothe a sense of disconnect from the natural world (or discomfort within soiled skin)

Notes from the garden shed

North Yorkshire, 2021 – present

I slept in the garden shed during the pandemic
    and decided to stay there: a little green shoot
plotting worries between wooden slats.
    I wake at the snuffle hour each time I stay the night:
a hedgehog leafs through gravel, and my brain,
    sticky with sleep, latches reassuringly onto the lock.
It's just before the fox hour, when the field catches fire,
    after which the ink spills and birdsong tangles in the trees.
It's nothing extraordinary: there's a picket fence
    by the strawberry patch still flaunting its price tag,
barcode scanned by each new dawn.
    I hear the hum of a television from the blaze of the house, too.
But as thistles loosen in this mud-starved brain
    seeds settle into script, into *strata*.

The geology of language

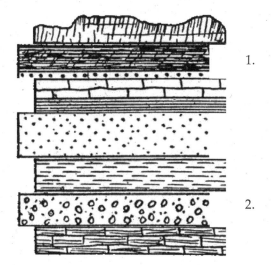

1.

2.

---

1. Poetry is pure strata: to dig through lines in
search of meaning roots us back to brown earth;
rekindles the prehistoric fire behind the urge
to forage, to scrape beneath the surface, to hope
from layer to layer.

2. The geology of language can also be studied
as a cross-section of race or class: the tongues
we bury or burn in the /grɑːs/.

Fieldlark

Picardy, France

I have a bomb in my backpack
         that can blast any minute:
a mausoleum of rust
         rumbled up by a plough.
Embalmed in metal and mud,
         the memory of war escapes:
commutes me back underground
         to eyes that flicker like electric cables.
Here, I do mind the gap
         between what it means
to lark and to lurk:
         its slippery slopes
are a bogspawned ditch,
         barbed with a fence
built in someone else's land.

Tongue-topography: field notes

After Camille Dungy

Question:

What colour is nature poetry?

Observation:

Reviewing more than 2,000 poems included in nature poetry anthologies and journals published from 1930 to 2006 — 80 years of the environmental literary canon — Camille Dungy finds only six poems by Black poets.

Hypothesis:

The landscape is white but the composition of text, and decomposition through reading, is a brown-fingered exercise. The legacy of language can be traced back to soiled earth.

Prediction:

Inside each letter rattles a grain of sand or soil — an origin story inscribed; seeds in the deepest, darkest layers of our animal brain. If these seeds are lying dormant, locked in linguistic code, all we need is a pen to bring their stories into bloom.

Data:

Example One

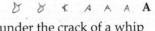

A was reared as an ox head under the crack of a whip
1800 BCE, muscle drafted into limestone walls at Wadi
el-Hol, Egypt. You can still trace the nose and two horns.
It took millennia for ठ to find its feet and stand tall;
plough sense to the surface of the mind's muddy fields.
Still ठ became A: the ox outgrew its cart. The letter
teaches my tongue to tug at its chain: to set fire to its pen
and run.

Example Two

B was scaffolded from a pile of papyrus reeds plucked
from the River Nile 2000 BCE, wet stems plaited into
a hieroglyph for home. You can still peer through the
two windows. Renovated by the Romans to a two-
storey triumph, B raised, as at Trajan's Column, whole
kingdoms of thought. Still B remains ⊐: the origin soaks
through. The letter urges me to flood white margins back
to marshland and mud.

24

Analysis:

An archery of resonance: each letter is a footprint, paw print, webbing, or a hoof, leading back to an ancient connection with the land[1]. These symbols leave a lingerprint of suspicion, framing language as the stringy green ties that will bond and brown me back to earth.

Conclusion:

There is a direct link between tongue and topography — language is silt-born, its ridge and furrow is brown. My tongue folds into its landscape with the faith of reading a map. It charts the contours of the only colour that can steer me home.

---

1. Symbols for a hunter's throwing stick, club, axe and bow splintered into C, F, Z and S. Meanwhile H, T and L first depicted a farmer's fence, cattle brand and prod, herding thought into paper folds. M still ripples its image of the sea, N the snake, Q the monkey with tail, U, V, W, Y wooden pegs and X crossed fish bones.

Mossary - II

bogspawn: debris spawned by muddied ground;
offspring of a black person (derogatory)

lingerprint: impression left on the imagination by the
lingering grasp of linguistic structures like words

mossary: glossary of eco-coinings; manifesto to fertilise
rather than flatten biodiverse thought-paths

roothood: roots or heritage holding selfhood in place
(or holding it back)

tongue-topography: landscape of language traced by
a tongue

The memory of water

After Jacques Benveniste

No matter how many times it is contaminated or cleaned,
     water carries a 'ghostly imprint'
of everything it dissolves.
     Each ripple encodes remembrance
through a memory-path of electrons:
     from river to roadside puddle,
each body of water is haunted
     by what it has lived before.

A nostalgia for my grandparents' farm
     has been soaked up second-hand:
I can feel the weight of everything lost,
     from the crumbling layers of history
to the cellophaned possibilities we never unwrapped.
     Stray dust lingers
like the half-finished draft of a dream.
     It eddies around the contours of memory
to map a sort of phantosphere:
     a ghostly realm of lost things
luring memory beyond its narrow sightline.

My family believe soil runs in the blood:
     the body carries a ghostly imprint,
pressed into generational strata.
     From pesticide run-off
to pigsty wastewater, I still ripple brownwards
     with the barnyard's muddied flow.
My blood encodes remembrance;
     the memory carries through.

Stonehenge

Salisbury plain, 3000 BCE

A ditch is dug with antler picks
and rigged with timber earthwork;
huge sarsens raised from mud-slicked holes
are lined with wooden stakes.
Beyond the trill of raven calls,
bronze-ladled feast and fire,
this ancient henge, greying flag,
waves passage through the seasons.
Each spring, tired pilgrims gather
to trudge across chalked grassland;
they'll sacrifice a dying sun
to rock to stream to stone.

Shardhenge

South London, 2008 CE

A building felled with bulldozers
is restored with metal glasswork;
huge salaries raised from oil-slicked pockets
are lined with political stakes.
Beyond the trill of video calls,
plastic-forked feast and wire,
this modern henge, gleaming flag,
waves passage through wealth and reason.
Each dawn, tired pilgrims gather
to trudge across charred underground;
they'll sacrifice a dying sun
to clock to screen to phone.

Poet as historical reenactor - I

Hastings, English Heritage event, 2023/1066

The castle is perched on a rocky sandstone crag
above a moat of weeds and shadow-fields of flint:
a subterranean memory-bank of history and hurt.

A banquet of burdock and wild boar is served
to the fingertip-march of a minstrel's plucked lute:
I am stationed in the silt-flushed basin below.

I have refused the role of the slave to be a soldier,
to brandish a sword that cuts deeper than words;
a shield that defends more than any pen could.

I billow between growing crowds and cracks
of moss-flanked flagstones; slip through
the silkscreen membrane of time like a ghost.

Chewing through the gristle of meat and millennia,
down to a skeletal truth, my skin maps with the silt
beneath my feet; a shared fretwork of stampede.

It can take years to adapt to the bulk of armour:
unless a re-enactor is already more ballast than body
and has battled the weight of history since birth.

Poet as historical reenactor - II

Beeston Castle, English Heritage event, 1265/2023

Today I am a nun and my wimple is falling down.
Roll up! Roll up! The sin of brown skin is on show!
I am wired to believe in a lower power — to kneel
to dirt for dirt's sake. My rivers of faith are brown.
If this poem is a prayer, and this page is an altar,
I worship my word not into its sacred white square
but into the quiet black soak of spilled ink or blood.

Mossary - III

phantosphere: beyond the earth's hydrosphere (water), biosphere (living things), lithosphere (land), geosphere (rocks) and cryosphere (ice) lies an unwritten layer of lost things (phantosphere)

shardhenge: pile of pottery shards; modern standing stone, skyscraper

shard sickness: wounding of spirit in the sustained presence of skyscrapers

silthood: cartographic kinship between silt and self; aesthetically in colour, historio-sociologically in hierarchical lowliness, ideologically in the history we both hold

earthescence: entangling of soil and self, or growing back into brownness; rooted in our inerasable status as creatures of the earth

Antonia Taylor

Antonia Taylor is a British Cypriot communications strategist and poet, currently working on her first collection of poems. Her work has been featured in publications including *Propel, Ambit, Harana, Marble Magazine, Dear Reader, Ink Sweat & Tears* and *Atrium,* and a new anthology of Reading poets from Two Rivers Press. Antonia also writes *The Conversation,* a weekly (ish) newsletter on thoughtful marketing and creative living. She lives in Reading with her husband and two teenage children.

"Love means you breathe in two countries."
– Naomi Shihab Nye

"It is one of the curiosities of Cyprus that things have always happened in the past or are going to happen in the future. The difficulty is to find the moment when they actually happen in the present."
– Lord Radcliffe, Constitutional Commissioner for Cyprus, 1956

When I came back to poetry after a hiatus of years, I hadn't intended to excavate my Cypriot identity; what it means to be bi-cultural or the legacy of war that has defined Cyprus' modern history. Once I started, I couldn't stop. I draw on the words of Palestinian-American poet Naomi Shihab Nye at the start of these poems. And it's this space – between two countries – Cyprus and the UK, the occupied north of the island and the free south, the past and present – that *Making a Big Deal of Stuffed Vine Leaves* exists in.

This selection of poems orbits around core concerns of loss, empire, religion, nation-states, inheritance, motherhood and patriarchal structures. My intention has been to interweave personal and collective history and memory, against the broader canvas of Cypriot history, as the daughter of refugees. I wanted to think about how this shapes identity, experience and perspective – the specific place of elsewhere that underpins the shared bi-cultural experience of both and neither.

These poems are for anyone who carries homesickness – perhaps a little nostalgia – with them, most days.

Antonia Taylor

Aubade for displaced echoes

Too many memories are inside of me and none
of them are mine. Sleep leaves like a country

in curfew. Occupy this hour, checkpoint the next,
ease my breath to the old harbour.

Lungs lined with my grandmother's loss,
an inheritance interrupted – sandstone, jacaranda seed,

every missed olive season, how she tried to stay;
scratch a flag into the mountain to trace

the Pentadaktylos skyline into forgetting.
How do you find a place to pray from?

I carry my exile like a lover,
or another bad election that breaks

the ebb of morning's tide. Face south and beg
for one last dream; it's always to return.

The Occupations

'The nightingales won't let you sleep in Platres.'
'Helen', George Seferis

Remember how the first boy you loved
held a gun to a nightingale's throat,
was it always going to end this way?
Most days you're done by sunrise.
Stand barefoot to watch dawn aching,
break a milk sweat & turn.
Late morning you miss your grandmother,
Her turquoise dress, kitchen heat.
All that she carried: a dowry, spilt salt,
rosewater, her bed still smooth,
the way she kept her desire
by the sink, to raise you homesick.

By three, your neck tells you no amount of guilt
can change the past. Welcome it. A houseguest.
Leave two fresh towels, lavender soap.
Tell me, is there a variation on partings?
That time in Paris: May heatwave, pavements
parasoled white, the cafe in Saint Sulpice.
Count commitments bare on your left hand.
Evening grass wet with regret, still,
you'd do it again. A fable of longing –

these sheets & songs & skin
urgent with night, tongueless.
Leaving is another language.

Empires everywhere fall

For my father

All your ghosts hang pale blue shirts. I pick the small comb,
drag debris like gunpowder across your woollen scent.

Make a pile of scratching moths on the bed
a siege of unfinished sentences & all your bad days.

A language you held at arm's distance. Like love,
you picked the easy parts that suited. I sift

through old receipts, two alphabets, the dusty harbour-town
kept in your bedside table. The end of God's name

seamed inside a jacket, sleeves you wrapped in dreams.
Somewhere you're watching Ayia Sophia flush red, turn east

& Constantinople still burning. I take your plaid scarves, now
smoky with years. You told me that when you were small,

soldiers searched animal skins for weapons. Your father's loyalty,
the childhood home I never saw. It was early spring.

I choose the forest green Aquascutum that made you feel
like London. Keep your passport, unapologetic as burnt-out foxholes.

I loved how you were unafraid to make every cut-through
in Bayswater yours. Remember that time I missed

work to meet you at the place behind Moscow Road?
You handed over the contract of homesickness,

a salted disease, stained the white tablecloth. Now it's in my marrow.
I pull jumpers, coats, from the shelf, ready for strangers.

All the parts of you I have no use for here. Let grief
fall through a pocket, loot an entire sky.

Don't die on a saint's day

Summer follows spring follows dust.
The priest spooned bread & burning

into my mouth. I kept it closed
just like he told me. To remember

the dead girl on each holy day
bring my witnessing back to her,

jasmine sweet on the evening's aniseed breath.
How the saints returned each 15th August.

Georgios. Konstantinos. Elias. They poisoned the dogs
& everything was closed. Reach for a fever dream,

wake a wall of heat. Have you ever asked your body
to forget the stone it can't put down?

Nothing grew that month except the fig tree
sinking with her purple fruit, sweet & screaming.

Counting

I've been counting days again
in wine glasses and carrot sticks.
Counting breath. Times I wake at night.
Eight mostly. Counting hours. Emails.
Pay cheques I pay myself. The small fires
I set to my body. When I was twelve
I read six hundred calories was how you
stayed loved. Sometimes I go over.
Counting the years since my father's face
drowned in bed lamplight. Suddenly
I need more hands for each winter.
Counting morphine shots. Those I misplaced.
His nightmares, counting times I saw him cry.
Twice. How long I'll live if I live as long
as my grandmother. She didn't know her birthday.
Perhaps late March, perhaps never.
                              Am I over halfway?
Counting the books my mother left
the morning they came for her. Saying it was a library,
a life. She took one son. And where are they now?
Their pages and days, pine leaves on a mountain
held for forty-seven Julys. Counting old loves. Cities
I haven't been to – Florence, Miami, Thessaloniki.
How much longer my children need me.
This takes no time, counting what I want,
a river and each Tuesday well spent.
When I reach beneath the sand to count
my memories, the sea snaps my hand.

Enough

Your daughter tells you
all constellations are arbitrary
she worries about your potential
the headline says oceans choke
on planes a new war started holy
it's been pouring since you were small
& now you're out of mascara
hurt your knees with the same prayer
forehead against the sycamore
this is where you buried God
when you came back
for him they'd cut it down
trip the doorstep's air
the way breathing catches you out
take only what you need &
sell what you can't hold
When did the piano become
such an extremist? The only way
you can sit opposite your friend
is if you look away
how are you a woman
with three dead friends?
four, if you count Elena brush a stray hair
from the desk – another & one more
notice you rake your ribs in your sleep
they discounted your ancestors till Monday
to tell you who you are – nothing
of your mother but the fingernails
of five empires scrape dirt
yesterday irises swelled
against the yellow
you wondered how to get to enough –
to pour empty the day
pull a dark sea
from the river's veined wrist.

Threads

When a friend said I carried pain lightly, I couldn't tell her it was sunlight that threads twenty-four ribs into a house for the missing. White as my grandmother's. The one they built after they took her home. In the camp opposite, the boy who squatted in puddles took his anger to a gun, paid off judges the way they slaughter birds – song thrush, skylark, turtle dove. My jean pocket threads, the dirty stars pigmenting my back from too many white Julys. How I wanted to scrape history from the map. Backstitched my father's handwriting beneath my left collarbone. Spat the ends like George showed me at the bar in Makariou, the one with the pool table and pistachio shells. He picked each one from my mouth. The threads they wound into my brother's spine & called it hope. Stretch fear over the hairline of your morning prayer. How do you unpick the memory of war? The place you're always leaving, an appointment grief won't miss. Each morning, you wove the ache into the sky, unseamed the blue with your teeth.

Jupiter hangs low on the horizon

November light grinds its teeth.
Variable stars, my daughter should be home.
Lately, there's been so much waiting
and last April I noticed crevices
in my neck. How these days,
I'm wanting more. Sunsets loosened
into oranges and pinks, fade
a too-ripe peach, its downiness
drawn back to stone, which later,
licked clean, I'll plant by the hydrangeas.
Imagine the velvet years I'll lie beneath mud,
perhaps then I'll notice rainfalls,
times I failed to hold her gaze.
Last night she showed me Jupiter –
how have I lived all these days
not knowing a sky-god lives in plain sight?
Among wet towels, football schedules,
unwelcome coffees with strangers.
Could I have her kept closer?
Turn Cassiopeia inside out at the mess
of it all, her five bright stars
hang the northern sky from an eyelash.

Effendi

Tonight, the heat tells me to choose
which language I dream in. Soon, all this
will be lost and we'll be the lucky ones.
Fields break bodies with failed negotiations;

this empire was anything but idle.
It funneled our gods and crushed our wheat.
Split us like bad apricots. From here,
we watch our sons unlearn each other –

how quickly a curfew becomes a war.
Effendi, scattering will mark our forearms
with checkpoints, make mountains
into enemy lines. When they tilted

your lemon cart on the Kyrenia Road
I wanted to kneel with you, dust traces
from our mingled blood, separated like oil,
like water; we waited for the forest fire.

I think of this on September nights, scent of jasmine,
warm bread, a whole city's betrayal
left hanging. Cicadas speak in ghosts,
crash their dry songs into carobs.

Spring lunchtimes, I knew you'd be waiting

by the gate of our old school,
the wrought iron one the Brits left.
Holding the hot chicken sandwich

with coleslaw nobody made like you.
Always too much mayo and your full weight
against the turquoise Hillman we all hated.

So in your body, that now you're not,
do the cypress trees still breathe
their clay? You always found people,

like when you met a childhood friend
with a whole war and an island
split in on itself and between you.

I was half in love with his son –
I heard he moved to LA now.
Why I didn't think *what a thing:*

to drive half-way across a small city
white with grief, all of you wrapped
in grease paper – sesame seed bread,

burgers for the boys, the orange carton
that gave me headaches. Turns out
I'm allergic and I never got to tell you.

Before your blood turned, that last trip home.
Could you find me now?
I'll share my lunch with you.

Take a bite, take half,
take the whole thing.
I saved it all this time.

Going back to the village

after Kyriakos Charalambides

History too has a hard time remembering –
sometimes you don't see the gun
                or shallow grave unturned for two lifetimes
left to wild dogs, nettles, amaranthine,
    what was too late disappeared unclaimed,
palms in rubble
    time pushes between invocations
Digeni, Sida –   I tried hard to leave
what I couldn't give back to beauty
            each failed memory, names in a dry mouth.

Mnimosino

When they say forty days what they mean is thousands.
All we had to do:
      pour your hours   into wintered ground.
        Tilt you back, again on the third day.
   Again, the ninth, the thirtieth,
            where the wheatberry fell and your mother lies,
                    an intercession of rain.
Saints watched us gather, faithless apostles
shaking hands & coats
throats raw as coins, sewn into memory rows
                at the front of the new church.
Unforgetting sings to where anemones cluster,
their eyes always go back dying.
      Leave God in the potholes,
      the white animal of sky.

Tell me how to grieve perfectly?

On the days they told me not to, I mourned that much better.
Faded to the clear pomace
          of memory's resin.

Pressed the pomegranate seed back   let it become many.
Eiona i mnimi.

Set fire to the olive grove.
The shivering air.

47

Be waiting

War won't sleep. Rivers turn to foxholes
dug by schoolboys, windows shutter
two to a grave. Orange groves shelter
silence. We stop to breathe Morphou's
distance – anemones reminding you
of the town you left burning. Their lilac necks
collapsed black pollen into my lungs
each February morning. Sometimes
the evil eye fails to make sunlight
from emergencies. When my father tended
his own grave, it was August. The radio
in Ayia Napa demanded a summer of love,
not the plane crash I squinted under.
The man who loved this sea so well told me
5 p.m. is the worst hour to break your own fall –
let wildfire burn water. The winter I was born in
abandoned the salt lakes where the dead vines grew.

Making a Big Deal of Stuffed Vine Leaves

Driving to the Turkish shop on the Oxford Road, I forget to avoid
Friday lunchtime. Maybe I wanted the call to prayer to wash me
with home. My body carries years of failed peace talks, aches to
negotiate a reconciliation. Flirt with the market owner, make it so
I still honour my ancestors, though I can't hold them. Try not to
think of their bones, their grains, unloved and do they know why
we don't go? Charm him with my three Turkish words: *günaydın,
haberler, ombesh* – he says it's plenty. I take the expensive jar and
don't tell him where you were from. Don't say these days I
mostly feel rinsed out. That I want to take the receipt and ask:
how do we forgive each other? At home, I line the heavy pan the
way I think you did. It seemed so easy. Press meat, pack rice, seal
onions. My mother says I make heavy weather of everything.
So I soften. I soften and I soften: just enough and not so much
that my eyes water. I hear our bodies can take more salt, that we
have this capacity. There's a photo of you on the internet from
after the war and I want to rip it down like the bougainvillea,
the white one you planted. I'm folding now – cinnamon, mint,
sixty oil-green parcels. I fold and I fold. Seawater and how many
Julys? Sometimes it seems I only exist in summer. Tonight, I'll
serve them to guests who never heard your story about the
watermelon field or watched you turn north to your endlessness.
Tonight, I'll swallow brine in my sleep.

Border Crossings

I tried again to pass through the Green Line. I wanted to offer my peace, a bag of sour cherries, but my father's ghost got in my eyes like he'd been waiting all summer.

At Eleftheria Square, by the old bus station, my sister told me to hide my phone. I bought a Diet Coke, apologised for the empire lingering in my blood.

A crescent moon and half-constellation scorched a flag into a mountainside. Δεν ξεχνώ peels homesickness from my lips.

Narrow streets hide what we forget in plain sight. Bullet marks daylight the windows to witness what we withhold.

I stayed for the call to prayer and lit a candle at Ayia Fanoromeni. Then I lit two.

Forgetting rips the vagus nerve of the city; they say you get used to the divide, the split in your body.

Last year the river flooded into the banks of the old town, to cleanse her torrents, *zeibekiko,* a missing persons list. Only the crows saw.

Where are you from?

I read that when they came, the soldiers looked for the forests first. Now I carry pines, oleander, my grandmother's olive trees, trace a stranger's pencil-line across a map of mistrust.

In Victoria Café we translated sweet honey and cornflour into a language we lost.

It's true that jasmine doesn't wilt in the heat of war. Even on the worst days, who can forget the scent of it?

At dusk, I asked the waiter to set another place.

Laura Varnam

Laura Varnam is the Lecturer in Old and Middle English Literature at University College, Oxford. She is working on a poetry collection inspired by the women of the Old English epic *Beowulf*. Her poems have been published in journals including *Bad Lilies, Banshee Lit, Berlin Lit, Dust Poetry, MIR Online, Osmosis Press, Wet Grain, Under the Radar* and in the anthology *Gods & Monsters*. Her poems have also been published with creative-critical essays in *postmedieval* and *Annie Journal*, and her academic work on late medieval literature and culture is widely published.

wiþ (prep.; adv.)

towards . to . in the direction of . with . against . over against . opposite to . from . by . near . unto . in the way of . part with . from . for . in return for . as payment for . for . in consideration of . in exchange for . in reward of . in answer to . as compensation for . in consideration of . on condition of . as a set-off . by the side of . compared with . in contrast with . contrary to . in opposition to . to weigh one thing with or against another . in comparison with . with a person . in respect to . through, . to rest on the arm . until

Hwæt! (That got your attention!) My Primers poems are inspired by Grendel's Mother, one of the three antagonists in the Old English epic *Beowulf*. Silenced, marginalised, and troublesome in the original narrative, my poems reimagine and give voice to the mighty mere-wife, exploring her life (and afterlife) in her own words. Drawing playfully on Old English vocabulary and imagery, the poems are framed by words that drop anchor in her story: *ær* (before) and *æfter* (after) her son's death at Beowulf's hands; as she moves *togeanes* (towards) her own inevitable fate; and *nu* (now), in our modern moment of reading, as we remember and celebrate her imaginative power. The poet Adrienne Rich declared that for women in particular, to reimagine or 're-vision' an old text was 'an act of survival' and my feminist adaptation project aims to restore to Grendel's Mother the dignity and recognition that she is denied by the original poem, not least by the absence of the mourning rituals that are reserved for men and not for so-called monsters. Who is Grendel's Mother and what stories might she tell? Let's listen to hwæt she has to say...

Laura Varnam

Hwæt! We have heard of the Spear-Danes
in days gone by, of the glory of the kings
of that people, how their noblemen performed
courageous deeds!

Beowulf, lines 1-3

Hwæt

Indeed.

We have heard of the Danes.
We never stop hearing about them.
Those death-and-glory Danes.
Them, their demons, and their glory-
days. Me, I'd prefer a little variation.

If you'd like to,
                    listen.

The hall-door is open:

        The mere-wife awaits her welcome.

Grendel's Mother gets a Voice

Grendles modor hleoðrode
(Grendel's mother sounded off...)

*

Now that I've finally got one
I don't know what to do with it.
It's quite a responsibility
don't you think?

Unlike a sword, it harbours no history.
I can hardly bear it. Where to begin?

*

I thought it would be mere-clear.
Diving into it – my boundless voice
pooling and swirling – that I'd discover
the mere-maid and not the story of the mere-maid.
I'd surface and suddenly –

I'm mauling my metaphors. This is new to me.

*

It's eyeing me up over there, lurking.
Like my son does. (Did.)
But I'm not going to natter on about him.
You had that covered.

Should I mother it? Warm it in my gullet?
Hoard it from harm. The sound of it,
hleoðrode, all tongues and italics
catches in my craw.

You'll be along soon to pocket it anyway.
Monsters have no voice-right.

Perhaps I should eat it.

Grendel's Mother addresses the Author

For all your bluster, warrior-poet,
Your puffed-up preening,
Your sword-swagger and shield-shuffling,
You still won't look at me.

Petrifying people? That's not my style.
It's not my stare that needles your braggadocio.
Any road, *you* started it.

Edging me out, making me your *mearcstapa*,
Your boundary-stalker, border-controller.
I never wanted to shoulder those lines.

You kettle me into the corners of your compounds,
Tuck me into the bottom drawer of your wordhoard,
Shushed and smothered by your fabrications.
Water-witch, she-wolf of the deep, troll-dam?

Give over. Don't be so nesh.

The Name of the Father

I was diving for oysters when it happened.

Ocean-borne, sea-sheltered,
I would unseal my mouth
to the sweet swell, take it all in.

Then a man came, fretting at flesh
and, dagger-drawn, stripped me to bone,
wolfed me, lip-smacking, raw,

shucked and sucked dry. He was off,
and I sank,
            clinging to sea-bed, tide-
spiralling, in-curling, shell-shocked.

Men do not know the name of Grendel's father.
Women do not need to know.

He made me a monster when he made me a mother:

my brine-baby, my salt-in-the-wound.

Gruesome She (*Genus Monstrum*)

Men are always trying to pin
me down like a specimen beetle.

As though marking out my edges
makes for security.
I've too many tentacles for that.

     (You bought that one? Of course
I don't. I do envy the squid though,
ink would be a game-changer).

They want to dissect and label,
     get the measure of me.

Trouble is, I prefer to keep myself
to myself and the reports get garbled.

What if I'm just a woman?

Not a monster, or a critter, or a spider-leg
bigfoot snakebite medusa-myth
ofwulf shebeast? *Hwaet* then?

Let's track down my entry
in their unnatural history:

     Mother, Grendel's: monster (female).
     Demonstrably: ogress, hag, troll-wife,
     ghastly dam, hell-bride, claws-and-talons
     in the night, witch-wife, ghoul, polluted creature...

A hideous tale, with a hideous tail. I could go on.
One of them even called me *post-human*. (If only,
I'd still be here, minding my business.)

I object to being the object of your riddle.
Saga hwæt ic hatte?[2]

---

2. 'Say what I am called' (from the Old English riddles).

mother and son on the moors
[during Grendel's reign of terror]

when we walk / I can contain him / just / shadow his stride / guide him
away from hearth hall horizon / my moth boy / drawn to their flame

my job to keep him safe / to hold him / to the fens and the fast places
but darkness wouldn't hold / never does

some nights I follow / force myself to face his handiwork / pick up
the pieces / slip them into the marshes / try to clean up

the moors / mind their own

after twelve winters / you'd think men would learn / they were biding
their time / so was I / *you must have known* / *turned a kind eye*

yes / love / try to keep it down when you come in / I can't bear the sound
they make / like babies

last night / they did what I could not / put a stop to it

I'll only manage it once / I fear

how would he go about it? / *jink down the moor* / *streak through the mist*
choke back the tears / he won't be missed

Aftermath I: Blood in the Mere

[Grendel's Mother speaks as her son bleeds out]

home is a bloodbath
the mere is glutted
  gelatinous

wound-fresh with
blood-of-my-blood

ulcerous, it roils

nis þæt heoru stow![3]
you can say that again

it makes my blood boil

while you drink-in victory
his blood cries out to me

I'm his only keeper
  and I'll follow his blood-line
to your oh-so-high hall
  to your blood brothers
                  your blood
      shed

---

3 *Nis þaet heoru stow!* ('That is not a pleasant place!' *Beowulf*, line 1372)

Æschere's Head

[Grendel's Mother explains]

I could say it wasn't my finest hour,
very unlike me, never done it before,
and the truth is, I hadn't and it wasn't,
but then I heard them – *the lesser horror
of a woman's warfare* – and well, that

was that. Heads would roll. (In actual
fact, it's harder to roll a head than you'd
think, even one as inflated as his). Hrothgar's
right-hand man, *runwita* and *raedbora*.
If you're so clever, Æschere, read this.

Ofer myrcan mor I manhandled him.
It's easier in one piece – and my son had
paved the way in that respect, no
lumps and bumps to catch their feet
when the path's well-oiled.

I knew it wouldn't take them long to catch
up (if not on). Even today they hide
behind surprise – *she came out of nowhere!*
– but my son didn't, did he? And I've always
kept a weather eye. Couldn't avoid it,

they plonked their bloody great meadhall
on my ridgeway (crossed a boundary
there!) but I digress. Back at my mere
I thought I'd stop them taking things
further – head them off, show them what's

at stake. I was only speaking their language.

----

runwita, rædbora: wise counsellor, personal advisor
ofer myrcan mor: over the murky moor

An Æfter Anum[4]

When they tell me that grief's
too cruel a companion, I scoff.
She's the only company I've got.

World is too wide and wheretofore
without you in it. It gapes.
There's no out-walking it.

From seabed to seashore,
earth's belly to mountain top
there is too, too much of me.

Grief taps my scapula
with calloused hand,
and tips her crown.

Take this cup
> *my shoulder-companion*
>> *it's yours to bear.*

---

4. *Beowulf*, line 2461. W.E. Leonard's translation is 'the lone one for the lost one'.

Do You Hear Me, Mere-Watcher?

[Grendel's Mother calls out as Beowulf approaches the mere]

I'll   suck   sap your strength
til your muscular trunk clunks to dirt
and the beetles in your stink-black
heart scuttle out reeling

I'll sink incisors into your sword-grip
scratch and gash til my name
claws up your throat   you retch up
untydre, wælgæst, aglæcwif

I'll give you female combat
and it isn't swordsong or wolfprowl

it's kite-shriek anger
          red with mother-blood

nostril-flared, nail-pinched
silence, being mistaken, taken
for a meek-mild maiden

when with my *fyrwit* I'll burn your
mangy bone-house to claggy ash
hurl your *guð-grædig* daggers
into my mere where they'll rust
and rest and no one will dare
to look for them and I'll be glad
          and I'll say so what

So fucking what?

----
untydre: evil progeny; *wælgæst*: slaughter-guest
aglæcwif: formidable female opponent
fyrwit: intelligence / curiosity (fire-wit)
guð-grædig: war-greedy

66

HWÆT! WAIT!

[Grendel's Mother to Beowulf during their fight]

Before you kill me   you need to hear this

> *the cave greens*
> > *leans to listen*
> > > *bone-dank*
> > > > *glistens*

1. This doesn't change anything.

2. Yes, you'll have another head to your name but what if you're too weak to handle it?

> *sword shudders, sweat sneaks betrayal*

3. You'll be lauded – monster-butcher! – but what if I'm the one they remember?

4. You'll remember me too. Eyes fat with my son, hair loosed for vengeance.

> *there's a woman in the water, watching*

5. Even when you say that Death took Grendel, He wears your face.

6. What if, when you head back to your homeland, I haunt you?

> *there's a woman in the water, witching*

7. And you can't help but tell them
     a) that I was *sorhful*, not *bolgenmod*,
                     overflowing not overreaching
     b) that my *gyrnwræc* made you yearn
     c) that our stories almost changed hands

                knock knock Beowulf won't you let her in

8. When I topped you, your dagger drooped like ice desperate to melt.

9. If you want that victory-blade, you'll have to turn your back on me.

10. When I'm dead, I'll be more dangerous.

               light swordflashes the lake
                     fingras burston

11. What kind of man are you?

                     cave-walls weep

        her last grave-gasp

Before you   kill me   tell   me:

        Will it have been worth it?

----
sorhful: sorrowful
bolgenmod: swollen with rage
gyrnwræc: grief-vengeance
fingras burston: fingers burst

Aftermath II: Dead in the Mere

[Grendel's Mother looks upon her son's headless body]

Even now I hear you calling:
Her, modor, her.

Is it cold there too? Do their crowing
eyes feast on your naked neck?

On their *fagne flor,* it weeps.

When his battle-light slit my bone-
locks, I thought: joined at *læst.*

Hwær eart þu, modor?

There's a reason their word for grief
is *torn.*

----

fagne flor: decorated/stained floor
læst: last, path or track
hwær eart þu, modor: where are you, mother?

Investigative Interview: The *Beowulf*-Poet

Case ref: Cotton Vitellius A XV
Re: The Actions of Grendel's Mother

Let's rewind, shall we? You're saying that *before* she fell (and we all know that she fell), these are the facts of the case: whether she wished to or not (can *you* speak to her motive?), she drew & she sat; she repaid & she carried – am I getting this straight? – she entered, she harmed (hold your horses there, sunshine), she clutched & held tight, she discovered she must [*to avenge, to protect, to avenge, to protect, to avenge*] (easy tiger, stick to the facts): she took off, she cut down, she came & she clung (sit tight, wait it out), she uncovered (with an eyeroll, no doubt), & how else she meant (don't get me wrong), she reached & became, & she came & she wished (and got carried away?) – she *had to* (you know that, don't you?), she remembered (*we* remember), & she lived. She *lived*. And that's it? That's all you've got?

Elegy for Grendel's Mother

Let me sing of her glory now:

how she came out of nowhere
and cut them down to size

how I'd never seen the like of her

how she got away from this place
and made them come to her

how she was only killed with her
own sword, not their puny daggers

how they were too scared to deadhead
her and carry her home to Heorot

how they can't stop talking shit about her

let me sing of her glory here:

before the woman becomes the myth

(how we are made to forget).

Swa cwæð eorðhus / thus spoke the earth-house

[Grendel's Mother's empty grave speaks]

I can't keep waiting for her
My *breostcofa* is empty

I must keep waiting for her
My *hordcofa* is barren

Idel ond unnyt
I'm bereft.

Hwær cwom mæg?
Hwær cwom modor?

I'm *modorcearig*

Eala!

my *banhus*

bone-light

----
breostcofa: breast-chamber
hordcofa: treasure-chamber
idel ond unnyt: idle/empty and useless
hwær cwom mæg, modor: where did the woman go, the mother
modorcearig: mother-anxious, mother-care-worn
eala: alas
banhus: bone-house

Acknowledgements and Notes

Jade Cuttle:
'The geology of language' – rock strata image: Ellsworth D. Foster ed., *The American Educator* (vol. 3) (Chicago, IL: Ralph Durham Company, 1921).

Antonia Taylor:
'Aubade for Displaced Echoes' refers to the *Pentadaktylos*, a part of the Kyrenia Mountains in the Occupied North of Cyprus.
'The Occupations' is in conversation with italicised lines directly from George Seferis' 'Helen', translated by Edmund Keeley.
'Back in the Village' – Digeni and Sida are sites where missing persons' remains from the 1974 war in Cyprus have been excavated for identification.
'Mnimosino' is the Greek Orthodox memorial service; it translates as "calling to mind." *Eiona i mnimi* translates to "memory eternal" and is repeated at the end of the service.
'Making a Big Deal of Stuffed Vine Leaves" references *günaydın, haberler, ombesh* which translate as *good morning, the news and fifteen* in Turkish.
'Border Crossings' – The Green Line is the demarcation line dividing Cyprus since 1974. *Zeimbekiko* is a Greek folk dance. Δεν ξεχνώ means "I don't forget" in Greek and is a core maxim for Greek-speaking Cypriot refugees.

Thank you to the editors of the following magazines where some of these poems were first published: 'The Occupations' in *Indelible Literary Journal,* 'Empires Fall Everywhere' and 'Enough' in *Dear Reader,* 'Counting' in *Propel Magazine* and 'Threads' in *Ambit Magazine.* Other poems have featured in *South, New Contexts, Blood Moon Poetry, Marble Magazine,* and *Riverside.*

Laura Varnam:

The definition of 'wiþ' is from the *Bosworth-Toller Dictionary of Old English*.

The title 'Gruesome She' is borrowed from Michael Alexander's translation of *Beowulf*.

'Grendel's Mother addresses the Author' and an earlier version of 'Hwæt' were first published in *The Oxford Magazine* 424 (Second Week, Michaelmas Term 2020) and then as part of my article 'Poems for the Women of *Beowulf*: 'A Contemporary Medieval' Project' in the academic journal *postmedieval*, 13 (2022), 105-21 (the former was entitled 'Grendel's Mother').

'*An Æfter Anum*' was first published in *Banshee Lit*, issue 14 (autumn/winter 2022). This poem is for E.C.

'*HWÆT! WAIT!*' is for R.D and N.M.
'Do You Hear Me, Mere-Watcher?' is for C.P.

I would like to thank Katie Hale and Jane Commane for their invaluable feedback on the poems and both Helen Barr and Robert Shearman for their generous encouragement and friendship.